A Gathering of Pearls

Karen Kay Knauss

COPYRIGHT © 2014

≈

A Gathering of Pearls

Karen Kay Knauss

All Rights Reserved

*No portion of this book may be reproduced in any manner whatsoever **without written permission** from the publisher, except for brief excerpts for review purposes.*

Cover Production: J. T. Harrison
Photographer: Danna Alane Anderson
Cover Design: Karen Kay Knauss

ptp
peachtreepress@pldi.net

2014
ISBN: 978-0-9895926-4-2

DEDICATION

If
a pearl represents a virtuous woman

If
a pearl symbolizes rare beauty
wisdom and serenity

If
a pearl is endowed with goodness
brilliance and strength

Then
the pearl chest of my heart is full

Roberta Phyllis Hall Knauss

Mother

and other precious pearls

Grandmothers and Sisters
Daughters and Granddaughters
Nieces, Aunts, and Cousins

Pearling Dhow

The Pearl

"The pearl holds the distinction of being the only gem that is formed within a living organism.

A pearl is made when an irritant finds its way into the soft tissue of the oyster. To protect itself, the oyster begins to cover the irritant with sheets of nacre, the smooth lining material that mollusks produce to covers the insides of their shells. Layer upon layer of nacre is applied to the irritant, producing, over a period of 1 - 3 years (or more), one pearl.

Pearls were considered among the most precious stones in the ancient world. In classical Rome, only persons above a certain rank were allowed to wear pearls. In the Americas, the Incas and Aztecs prized pearls for their beauty and magical powers.

For centuries the pearl was only known as the "Margarite", the Greek word for pearl; margarite is the name of the oyster that produces pearls found in the Persian Gulf and Red Sea. It was not until the King James Version of the Bible that the term pearl was used."

Smith's Bible Dictionary

PEARLING TERMS

Pearler - ancient pearl diver

Pearler - ancient pearling boat or dhow

Chitini - one who places the value on pearls

Pearl Oyster - oysters that form pearls

Natural pearls - pearls created naturally

Cultured pearls - pearls created by man

Faux pearls - pearls made of wax and pearl powder called essence d 'orient

Rope - rope on which divers descend and ascend; a large rock is attached in descent

Nacre - mother-of-pearl layers that form a pearl

Mantle - part of oyster that secretes nacre

Luster - brilliance; defines beauty and value

Mother-of-pearl - inside of mollusk shell

Seedbed - an area of pearl growth

Seed Pearl - a very small, often imperfect pearl of lesser value

Pearl Knot - a knot tied between pearls on string to keep them from touching

Sea Chest - a chest storing the captain's pearls gathered at harvest

Yam - God of the Sea

Matching - pearls of like size and value

Nakhutha - captain of a pearling boat

REFERENCES INTRODUCE POEMS

POEMS

Title	Page
Eve	2
Jochebed	3
Hannah	6
Naomi	8
Deborah	9
Sisters of Jesus	12
Jemima, Kezia, Kerenhappuch	14
Huldah	16
Anna	18
Elizabeth	20
Bithiah	22
Miriam, the Sister	24

Miriam, the Prophetess	26
Vashti	28
Rebekah, the Beloved	30
Rebekah, the Matriarch	32
Dinah	34
Leah	36
Rachel	38
Ruth	40
Jezebel	42
Sarah	44
Hagar	46
Bathsheba	48
Tamar	50

Delilah	52
Esther	54
Mary	56
Mary Magdalene	58
Martha	60
Mary of Bethany	62
Abigail	64
Jael	66
Asenath	68
Dorcas	70
Candace	72
Joanna	74
Sheba	76

Sherah	78
Rahab	80
Achsah	82
Lydia	84
Phoebe	86
Lois	88
Eunice	90
Five Sisters	92
Zipporah	93
Elisheba	96
Tekoah Woman	98
Priscilla	100
Athalia	102

Bilhah	104
Nameless Slave Girl	106
Thecla	108
Sophia	110
Michal	112
Judith, the Hittite	114
Junia	116
Rhoda	118
Judith, the Courageous	120
Author's Page	124
Author's Works	126

women of rare distinction

Like the pearl divers of old,
my research has taken me deep into
the sea of time to gather rare pearls—

a treasure of unique personalities
from the familiar, and not so familiar
women of antiquity.

With the artistry of poetic voice,
sensitivity, and style, their challenges
to overcome social and moral injustices
similar to those of the modern woman
have been revealed—

gender and racial prejudice, abuse
inequality, rape, dishonor, and betrayal.

With the artistry of analogy the
history of an ancient pearling industry
has been woven into their remarkable
life experiences— thus exemplifying each
one's strength, wisdom, and beauty.

The women— like pearls
have been gathered together on the
silken thread of poetry.

all
with luster and symmetry

each
strung lovingly
with pure silk thread
knotted tightly

together
in the harmony
of beauty and form—

Karen Kay Knauss

A Gathering of Pearls

Karen Kay Knauss

Genesis 3:20

And Adam called his wife's name Eve, because she was the mother of all living.

Eve

Around her slender, sacred neck
beneath the haloed hollow
lay jewels of rare distinction

Mother of us all
adorned with elegant
pearls of many colors
black, white, yellow, red

all
with luster and symmetry

each
strung lovingly
with pure silk thread
then knotted tightly

together
in the harmony
of beauty and form—

like pearls of descendancy
cascading from her heart

Jochebed

The gray solitude
of early morning
was broken as the
red dust of dawn
drifted slowly
through a blue sky

It drifted upward
from the bottom
of a dark horizon
like a rising sadness
burning in the depth
of a mother's heart

This day would mark
an end to the layering
of a mother's love—
the beginning of a new
life for her precious pearl

*Have I given him the
luster of a beautiful coat*

*Have I given him the
inner strength to endure*

The pearl diver
descended— as she knew
he surely would

He drifted upward
through the blue water
like the red dust of dawn

then laid the pearl into
royal and loving hands

Exodus2:3

*And when she could no longer hide him, she took for
him an ark of bulrushes....and she laid it in the flags
by the river's brink.*
Ex. Rabbah 1:26
Jochebed nursed Moses for twenty-four months.

I Samuel 1:11

And she vowed a vow, and said, O LORD, if thou.....wilt give unto thine handmaid a man child, I will give him unto the LORD all the days of his life.

Hannah

From my heart
I implored—
I will bear the babe
I will nurture the child

From my blessed womb
from the cradle of his youth
I will return a pearl of wisdom

We will rise up in obedience—
Samuel and me

This promise
I make unto Thee

Because I have asked
for him from the Lord

Ruth Rabbah 2:5

...she was named Naomi "because her actions were fine and pleasant"

Ruth 4:14 KJV
And the women said unto Naomi, Blessed be the Lord, *which hath not left thee this day without a kinsman, that his name may be famous in Israel.*

Naomi

For loss of a husband
Ruth followed Naomi
For gain of this daughter
a grandson was given—

after many years in grief

For loss of comfort
a marvelous pearl becomes
For gain of a pearl
a remarkable gift is given—

after many years in the sea

Obed, the grandson of Naomi
Jesse, the gift of Obed
David, the gift of Jesse
David, a remarkable gemstone—

after many years in Israel

Deborah

Deborah sat beneath a palm tree
it stood as a certain witness to
her sense of reason and justice

The children of Israel came to her
for wisdom and counsel— in despair
and fear of Sisera's chariots of war

They were weary of defeat in battle—
forced to hide in Canaan's barren hills
where neither milk nor honey flowed

She knew of the Israelites' defiance
she remembered the Lord's promises
she walked in paths of righteousness

Like pearls strung on a lovely necklace
with silk thread holding them together
and pearl knots keeping them secure

the careless children became tarnished
weakened by their unraveling fears
and loosened by gradual disobedience—

for worship of Baal's idolatrous gods
for harsh oppression of the Canaanites
for lack of faith and true commitment

Deborah sat beneath a palm tree
God called out to his chosen Prophetess
to restore Israel— *to restring his pearls*

Judges 5:7

Village life ceased.....
Until I, Deborah, arose,
Arose a mother in Israel.

Mark 6:3

Is not this the carpenter, the son of Mary, the brother of James and Joses, and of Judas and Simon? And are not his sisters here with us?

Sisters of Jesus

The nameless sisters
of the Savior
will remain like
pearls in the
depths

   of the

      sea

More rare with time
lustrous and desirable
while eluding the
diver's hand in the
depths

   of the

      sea

Job 42:15

And in all the land were no women found so *fair as the daughters of Job: and their father gave them inheritance among their brethren.*

Jemima, Kezia, and Kerenhappuch

Three daughters—
three Pearls for Job

Jemima, the first

born in the luster of
sunlight that grew
brighter and brighter
with each new day

Kezia, the second

born in the fragrance
of sweet herbs that
soothed and healed
the afflicted flesh

Kerenhappuch, the third

born in the glory
of a jeweled crown
that signified restoration
of honor and dignity

II Kings 22: 18-20

But to the king of Judah which sent you to enquire of the L<small>ORD</small>, thus shall ye say to him...Because thine heart was tender...Thine eyes shall not see all the evil which I will bring upon this place.

Huldah

She spoke with words of knowledge
to women, mothers, and daughters
she spoke with words of prophecy
to King Josiah in the city of Jerusalem

A found book of law warned of curses—
Josiah feared and commanded his priest

Go ye, inquire of the LORD for me
For the people and for all Judah

Remarkably sensitive
strong and sought after
Huldah was like a rare pearl—
created by a living being
imparting a mantle of hope
and salvation from destruction

Huldah's prophecy that Josiah
would be spared for his goodness
was known to all Judah—

it brought forth a righteous revival

Ambrogio Lorenzetti
"Presentation of Jesus in the Temple" 1342
Tempera on Panel

Luke 2:38

And she coming in that instant gave thanks likewise unto the Lord, and spake of him to all them that looked for redemption in Jerusalem.

Anna

Lorenzetti dressed Anna
in a long purple robe and placed
a golden halo around her head

The prophetess stood resolute
next to Mother Mary's babe
held gently by the aged Simeon

Anna extends her gestural hand—
points to the infant and proclaims
His name written on a sacred scroll

Lorenzetti, like generations of old
knew Anna for her enduring faith
as she served in the Temple of God

Like the master seeker of rare pearls
she had searched years for the Savior
through scrolls of law and prophesies

It was Anna who
professed the worthiness
of the infant's holy name

Luke 1:13

But the angel said unto him, Fear not, Zacharias: for thy prayer is heard; and thy wife Elisabeth shall bear thee a son... thou shalt call him John.

Elizabeth

Years in the sea
the closed shell lay
in quiet obedience
to the laws of nature

Layer upon layer
of nacre-like faith
promised Elizabeth

a pearl

Barrenness was broken
with the gift of

 a child

growing and waxing strong—
till he came forth from the
desert in luster and matching
with the one they called Messiah

Elizabeth rejoiced

Ex. Rabbah 1:24

Thus, when the daughter of Pharaoh opened the ark, Moses, unlike other babies, did not cry. The angel Gabriel immediately came and hit Moses so that he would cry, thereby arousing the compassion of the daughter of Pharaoh.

Bithiah

She opened the cradle shell
of bulrushes, slime and pitch
and gazed upon a pearl

She gathered it gently from
the flags and waters of the Nile

lifted the babe for her own

then hid the mother cradle away—

lovingly

Exodus 2:4

And his sister stood afar off, to wit what would be done to him.

Miriam, the Sister

Miriam stood at a distance
watching after the babe
born in the darkened days
of Pharaoh's death decree

She watched that he
might not drown—

*or be drowned
in the Nile*

He lay in a small
woven basket placed
in shallow, reedy water
where he cried aloud
for the taste of his
mother's sweet milk

Miriam watched that he
and all the children of Israel
might not drown—

*or be drowned
in the Red Sea*

Exodus 15:20

And Miriam the prophetess, the sister of Aaron, took a timbrel in her hand; and all the women went out after her with timbrels and with dances.

Miriam, the Prophetess

Miriam stood at a distance

The Lord kept her there for
seven days of refinement—
like a blemished pearl

For mercy petitioned
by Moses, the chosen Prophet
a curse of leprosy was
lifted from the Prophetess

Miriam
took a timbrel in her hand

then
she danced merrily
in praise of the Lord—

the Master of pearls

Ester 1:10

Therefore, if it pleases the king, let him issue a royal decree and let it be written in the laws of Persia and Media.....that Vashti is never again to enter the presence of King Xerxes.

Vashti

The queen placed a value
on herself, as ancient
pearlers on their jewels

She was lovely

though the drunken king
cared not for her virtue
nor for her distinction

Heartlessly—

he cast her back
into
    the
        sea

Genesis 24:67

And Isaac brought her into his mother Sarah's tent, and took Rebekah, and she became his wife; and he loved her.

Rebekah, the Beloved

Abraham cast the rope
into the sea of his homeland

Like the pearl diver of old
his servant prayed for
a prosperous harvest in the
land of Mesopotamia

Rebekah went down
to the well and drew water

then
drew for the servant
and the camels of Abraham

Rebekah was a gift
like a pearl from the sea—
given to Isaac, son of Abraham

and he loved her

Genesis 24:60

And they blessed Rebekah, and said unto her, Thou art *our sister, be thou* the mother *of thousands of millions, and let thy seed possess the gate of those which hate them.*

Rebekah, the Matriarch

Twenty years she waited
upon the Lord to bestow
her brothers' blessings—
to become a mother

And when the shell opened
two pearls lay within

distinctive in appearance

distinctive in Rebekah's favor

distinctive in the seed of

Abraham

Isaac

and

Jacob

Genesis 30:21

....and then Leah had a daughter and she named her Dinah.

Dinah

Chitini set the value of a pearl
like pearlers set boundaries
in the sea

Like the LORD set marriage laws
in Jacob's tent

Dinah was taken from the sea
from the layering Mother-of-Pearl

too soon

She was defiled by a stranger in an
unfamiliar land called Shechem

Still
Jacob kept the seed pearl

He carried Dinah into Egypt
with his family—
and her name was forever
written on his page

Genesis 29:30

So Jacob went in to Rachel also, and he loved Rachel more than Leah

Leah

Tender eyes often
filled with her tears

for Jacob found
no favor with Leah—

*nor a teardrop pearl
with the buyer's bid*

Still
she was loyal
and her inner luster
pleased Jehovah well

Mother of Judah
and revered Matriarch

Leah lies in the holy
Cave of Machpelah

with favor—

forever beside Jacob

Genesis 29: 10-11

.....when Jacob saw Rachel, he went near.....and kissed Rachel, and lifted up his voice, and wept.

Rachel

To the depth
of fourteen fathoms
divers will descend
to gather a rare pearl

To the length
of fourteen years
Jacob labored
to gather Rachel

All that a pearl is—
Rachel was to Jacob

Beautiful and desirous
a treasured gift
of goodness and posterity
a symbol of the soul—

and Jacob's love

Ruth 1:22

So Naomi returned, and Ruth the Moabitess, her daughter in law, with her, which returned out of the country of Moab: and they came to Bethlehem in the beginning of barley harvest.

Ruth

Unto the pearlers
there is a season
to harvest in the sea

Unto the reapers
there is a season
to harvest in the field

Ruth gathered golden grain
fallen along the barley rows
as ancient law would allow

and even more—
when the favor of Boaz
was bestowed upon her

She ate of his bread
gathered throughout his fields

and even more—
from the bundled sheaves
that he allowed

Boaz knew her goodness
he became her redeemer
he took her for his wife

Revelation 2:20

.....I have a few things against thee, because thou sufferest that woman Jezebel, which calleth herself a prophetess, to teach and to seduce my servants to commit fornication, and to eat things sacrificed unto idols.

Jezebel

With no reflection
from the soul within
or
luster to the eyes of
one who valued pearls

Jezebel was not true

With no layering
of precious nacre
or
years of refinement
in the ancient sea

Jezebel was worthless

With no pleasure
from her touch
or
safety in the
Master's sea chest

Jezebel was cast away

Genesis 18:11

Now Abraham and Sarah were old and well stricken in age; and it ceased to be with Sarah after the manner of women.

Sarah

With every new spring
Sarah witnessed life—

marking yet another
sad and barren year

without a child

With every new spring
the oyster knew life—

defining yet another
aging ring of growth

without a pearl

Though none should
speak of hopelessness
in the presence of Yam

the God of the sea

nor
in the presence of Yahweh

the God of Abraham

Paragraph 146 of Hammurabi's Code,
Ancient Mesopotamian Legal Code:

If a man has married a priestess and she has given a slave girl to her husband and she bears sons, if that slave girl goes about making herself equal to her mistress, her mistress may not sell her; she may put the mark of a slave on her...

Genesis 16:4

And he went in unto Hagar, and she conceived: and when she saw that she had conceived, her mistress was despised in her eyes.

Hagar

The splash of oars
across the calm sea
kept rhythm with the
pearlers joyous song

in the lateness of the day

and the moon was full

Sarah's gift to Hagar
was given in one accord—
to become Abram's wife
for the blessing of his children

yet
there was no harmony

in the lateness of the day

and Hagar's heart was empty

2 Samuel 11:2-4

...from the roof he saw a woman washing herself;
and the woman was very beautiful to look upon.
And David sent messengers, and took her;

Bathsheba

Among the daily catch
one pearl above all others
may blind the diver's eye

he may watch the captain
from afar— conspiring
to take the precious pearl

Bathsheba's beauty was rare
and David watched her bathing
though she was not his by law

If the captain looks away—
or if he dies— the King may claim
the pearl he desires as his own

David and Bathsheba
were punished for their selfish
and licentious sin

they could not imagine
the bitterness of their tears

nor
the sweetness of God's mercy

ISRAEL (Mosaic Law)

If a man meets a virgin who is not betrothed, and seizes her and lies with her, and they are found, then the man who lay with her shall give to the father of the young woman fifty shekels of silver, and she shall be his wife, because he has violated her. He may not divorce her all his days.

2 Samuel 13:12-14

And she answered him, Nay, my brother, do not force me.....but, being stronger than she, Amnon forced her, and lay with her.

Tamar

Tamar was innocent—
she was the obedient
daughter of David

To Amnon, her brother
she was *a fair sister*
naive and helpless

he deceived her
he raped her
he dishonored her

Tamar put ashes
on her head—

tore off her colorful
virgin robe—

and cried in desolation

To Absalom, her brother
she was *a beloved sister*
violated and heartbroken
She was worthy of justice—

Amnon would have to pay

Judges 16:4

And it came to pass, that he loved a woman in the valley of Sorek, whose name was Delilah.

Delilah

When Samson walked
among the Philistines

it was the *illusion* of
a pearl that beguiled
his credulous heart—

When he held
Delilah in his arms
his passion was

the first to deceive

Delilah's iridescence
revealed a callous
and ever-changing heart—

the second to deceive

Esther 4:16

Go, gather all the Jews that are present in Shushan, and fast ye for me.....and so will I go in unto the king, which is not according to the law: and if I perish, I perish.

Esther

Esther and Mordecai—
two pearls on a strand
in the land of Shushan

held together by the
pearl knots of God's law

For all her husband's favor
and declarations of love
Esther feared for her people
and Xerxes' rejection—

she feared for her life
by the King's own decree

yet twice he held out the
golden septre in adoration

Esther knew if the strand
of her people was broken
a few might fall— though
many would be saved by
the pearl knots of God's law

The pearl knots held

Luke 1:38

And Mary said, Behold the handmaid of the Lord; be it unto me according to thy word.

Mary

The angel Gabriel
came into the presence
of Mary, the virgin

he spoke of a great testing
of her unwavering faith
of her perfect obedience—

for the rarest of blessings

The intruder comes
into the oyster shell
deep in the Sea of Galilee

it causes a great layering
of Mother-of-Pearl
in obedience to nature's law—

For the rarest of pearls

Mary was faithful and obedient
though her suffering was great

She knew the rarest of blessings

She was the rarest of pearls

Mark 16:9

Now when Jesus was risen early the first day of the week, he appeared first to Mary Magdalene

Mary Magdalene

With a vigilant eye
the captain guarded
the precious pearls
within the sea chest—
on the shores of Galilee

while
Mary Magdalene
watched the tomb of
the precious Savior—
in a garden near Golgatha

Mary would be the first
to see the opened chest
to witness the greatest
treasure of all mankind—

the gift of everlasting life

John 11:5

Now it came to pass that he entered into a certain village: and a certain woman named Martha received him into her house.

Martha

Jesus often walked
the eastern slopes of
the Mount of Olives
to visit the tranquil
village of Bethany

Martha's home was there
a place to rest—

she welcomed Him

Martha prepared supper
for the Son of God—

she served Him

Martha called him Lord
When Lazarus died—

she worshipped Him

John 11:32-35

Then when Mary was come where Jesus was, she fell down at his feet...When Jesus saw her weeping....he groaned in the spirit, and was troubled.....Jesus wept.

Mary of Bethany

Mary left her work
and listened to His words—
the sister who sat

at the feet of Jesus

Mary poured rich ointment
and dried His feet with her hair—
the sister who worshipped

at the feet of Jesus

Mary ran to Him
in grief of Lazarus' death—
the sister who cried

at the feet of Jesus

I Samuel 25:32

*And David said to Abigail, Blessed be
the* L{\sc ord} *God of Israel, which sent thee this day*

Abigail

For fear of needless bloodshed
for futility of revenge after battle
Abigail did prepare in haste

two hundred loaves
two bottles of wine
five sheep ready dressed
five measures of parched corn
one hundred clusters of raisins
and two hundred cakes of figs

For favor from the God of Israel—

who sent the handmaid
with gifts of persuasion
with words of ancient prophesy
and wise counsel—

David hearkened to
the voice of Abigail
and many lives were spared

Judges 5:24

Then sang Deborah and Barak the son of Abinoam on that day, saying....Blessed above women shall Jael the wife of Heber be.

Jael

When Sisera asked for deliverance
Jael gave him deception

When Sisera asked for water
Jael gave him milk

When Sisera asked for respite
Jael gave him death

Jael's faith was strong
her skills were keen

as she drove the tent spike
into his temple—

her courage was unwavering
her name was spoken with praise

for her love of Israel

JOSEPH AND ASENATH

Accordingly, be of good cheer, Asenath, the virgin and pure, for lo! thy name hath been written in the book of life and shall not be blotted out forever;

E.W. Brooks

Asenath

We know of Asenath
what we choose to know—
for her name has been
written as well on secular
pages from ancient times

Though three times
the sacred pages spoke of
a virgin, a wife, and a mother—

none had revealed
her beauty and goodness
her love for Joseph
her prayer and conversion

None spoke of the ageless
story of an April love
nor of the bees with wings of
iridescent purple, blue, and gold
that kissed her lips and evil away

None spoke of the warm
and lingering embrace
she shared with Joseph—

others penned Aenath's page
And who can say it is not so

Acts 9:36-43

there was at Joppa a certain disciple named Tabitha, which by interpretation is called Dorcas: this woman was full of good works and almsdeeds

Dorcas

The moon is full
rising in a cold sapphire sky
I linger in its radiance

I am in awe

Dorcas comes as well
into a sister's darkened day
I linger in her compassion

I am calm

Benevolent hands
guide her nimble needles
while stitching a loving coat
I linger in her comfort

I am warm

Dorcas is full
reflecting divine light
I linger in her presence

My soul stirs within

History of the Christian Church, Schaff, Philip

Strabo mentions a queen of Meroè in Ethiopia, under that name, which was probably, like Pharaoh, a dynastic title.

Acts 8:27

and, behold, a man of Ethiopia, an eunuch of great authority under Candace queen of the Ethiopians, who had the charge of all her treasure, and had come to Jerusalem for to worship,

Candace

No one thought to write
your name, as if it were
inconsequential at the time—
Candace queen seemed enough

Luke said no more on the sacred pages

Nineteen centuries since
I wander between Luke's lines—
like open fields once thought
the faraway ends of the earth—
to find your name

Amanitare

I walk along Ethiopian roads
lined with lovely blue lobelia
and mauve and pink clover

Beyond a field of yellow daisies
I catch a glimpse of the red wolf—
he leapt as if with wings

I admire your warrior power
I marvel at your golden jewels
I look into your large curious eyes

I wish that Luke were here

Luke 24:10-11

It was Mary Magdalene and Joanna, and Mary, and other women that were with them, which told these things unto the apostles. And their words seemed as idle tales, and they believed them not.

Joanna

To think an oyster idle
is to be mistaken

or that it only clings
to a rock in simplicity

or because thousands
are opened without
a single pearl —

that none should be regarded

Eleven men who walked
with Jesus were also mistaken

They wondered about in
doubt and disbelief of
Joanna and Mary, Susanna
Mary Magdalene

and other women from Galilee

the quiet
  simple
    believers

Hans Holbein, the Younger

"Solomon and the Queen of Sheba"

Pen and brush in bistre and grey wash, heightened in white, gold, and oxidized silver with red and green watercolour, Royal Library, Windsor Castle. 1534/1535

Elmer Towns

Sources outside the Bible suggest that the Queen of Sheba conceived a child in secret with King Solomon, while some Bible commentators have suggested that the nameless woman in the Song of Solomon is the Queen of Sheba.

Sheba

In an intricate work of art
Hans Holbein reveals a
longstanding legend of the
captivating Queen of Sheba

Pen and brush washed in grey
enhanced with silver and gold
imagery as rich as Sheba's
gifts of spices, balsam, and gold—
as intriguing and mysterious
as the ageless love story of
Queen Sheba and King Solomon

Was she real, was her name
Nikaulis, did she bear him a son
was she as "dark and lovely"
as the one in Solomon's song—

or is Sheba the figment of
the romantic's imagination

or the pillar of a necessary
and popular political will

or, simply a Christian heroine—

How grey is Holbein's Sheba

The Hittites: Their Inscriptions and Their History,
Vol. 2 Chapter IX

Zoheth had the good fortune to marry Sherah....She is said to have built Beth Horon, the nether and the upper, and Uzzen Sherah.

Sherah

The ancient trade route
lay like a pearl garland
across the plains of Ajalon

winding through your
ancient cities— placed like
crowns upon the hilltops—

with verdant valleys below
and the Jordan to the east

In the western distance one can
clearly see a white sandy shore
trimming the blue waters of the
Mediterranean Sea—

while standing
on an ancient Roman road

searching for the image of
your face, the color of your eyes
the rareness of your strong spirit

Joshua 2:18

Behold, when we come into the land, thou shalt bind this line of scarlet thread in the window which thou didst let us down by: and thou shalt bring thy father, and thy mother, and thy brethren, and all thy father's household, home unto thee.

Rahab

Deep into the land of Jericho
two spies found their way to
Rahab's door, to the safety

behind the walls of her inn
beneath the stalks of her flax
below the window by her rope

Rahab's scarlet cord was woven
with flax as strong as her faith
in the God of heaven and earth

For her kindness and discretion
she asked for a favor in kind—
that she and her family would

be spared when the walls of
Jericho would fall down with
the wrath of Joshua's God

Rahab let down the scarlet rope
she heard the trumpets sound—
she received the promise of life

Joshua 15:19

Give me a blessing; for thou hast given me a south land; give me also springs of water.

Achsah

To his daughter Achsah
Caleb gave the desert land
of Negev that lay in the south

True, it was a dry and
rocky desert land

but luscious lilies, tulips
red anemones and colorful flora
thrived and captivated

waterfalls spilled over
and caves bore markings of intrigue

Gazelle, leopard and
ibex moved with ease across
Wadi beds and rocky terrain
and onager stayed at a distance

Still, Achsah knew well the
wealth of spring waters—

for her flocks of sheep
for her farms and livelihood—
for her footprints in the sand

Acts 16:14

And a certain woman named Lydia, a seller of purple, of the city of Thyatira, who worshiped God, heard us: whose heart the Lord opened, so that she attended unto the things which were spoken by Paul.

Lydia

The seller of purple cloth
walked down to the river
that flowed through Philippi
in ancient Macedonia

to pray with Paul
to be baptized and testify
to become the revered

Saint Lydia

Now blessings are beseeched
with a kiss to an iconic face
and praise to her holy name

Lydia had the luster of
a remarkable pearl—
reflecting the image of God
wherever she turned

She had an inner glow
of warmth and kindness
with a deep persuasion that
softened unbelieving hearts

Lydia was indeed
a certain woman

Romans 16:1-2

I commend to you our sister Phoebe, a deacon of the church in Cenchreae. I ask you to receive her in the Lord in a way worthy of his people and to give her any help she may need from you, she has been the benefactor of many people, including me.

Phoebe

Like pearls scattered in the sand

A few enduring words
were thoughtfully scratched
onto the torn papyrus

With an earnest plea, Paul
penned his praise for Phoebe—
a worthy saint

Or was she a sister
A deaconess
A servant
A succourer
Or a trusted courier

The paper leaves carried in her hands
long years and ancient languages ago
declared her devotion and benevolence

There with Paul's written words
hidden deep in the sands of Egypt —
with any choice of interpretation

the image of Phoebe
glistens in perpetuity

2 Timothy 1:5

I call to remembrance the unfeigned faith that is in thee, which dwelt first in thy grandmother Lois, and thy mother Eunice;

Lois

Upon a stone foundation
the walls of sun-baked bricks
were laid in staggering rows
with a small window for light—

each held in place with clay mortar

Lois built another house

Her foundation was the gospel
the bricks were tempered with love
that weathered the storms of life
with a clear and radiant light
from one generation to another

each held in place with unyielding faith

Lois lived in this house

2 Timothy 3:14-15

And that from a child thou hast known the holy scriptures,

Eunice

Of mothers
who taught their sons
the ancient law

who bade them farewell
when called upon to serve

who suffered at their deaths—
still believing

Eunice was one

She exemplified
faithfulness and obedience
in her humble home at Lystra—

trust and commitment
as her son ministered
in faraway places—

strength and endurance
when death at the hands
of non-believers fell upon
her beloved son

Numbers 27:6-7

And the LORD spake unto Moses, saying, The daughters of Zelophehad speak right: thou shalt surely give them a possession of an inheritance among their father's brethren; and thou shalt cause the inheritance of their father to pass unto them.

Five Sisters

Five pearls of wisdom
were found in the land
west of the Jordan River

Zelophehad had fathered
no sons, only five daughters
Mahlah, Noah, Hoglah
Milcah and Tirzah

With layers and layers
of nacre the pearl becomes
lustrous and strong—
with years and years
of obedience the sisters
became wise and strong

As they petitioned Moses
for their father's inheritance
they were aligned perfectly
with one another

Like the crystals of nacre
that reflect a rainbow
of light and color—
the sisters reflected
the wisdom of ancient
and enduring law

Zipporah

Have the written words
tarnished your brilliant luster
to an undeserved dullness

because you once had
little favor of the ancients
as of the reproving Miriam—

because your dark-skin color
was not the same as those who
claimed their kinship to Moses—

because your unfamiliar faith
from a foreign land was strange
and to them unacceptable

From searchings deep into
the sea of time, come answers
raised up within the diver's net

pearls of many colors were
found more rare than the
most precious of diamonds—

the skin of Miriam was
the skin cursed with leprosy—
for prejudice and impudence

God placed no blame
upon his daughter
Zipporah—

in any of the written words

Numbers 12:1

Miriam and Aaron spoke against Moses because
of the Cushite woman whom he had married

Exodus 6:23

And Aaron took him Elisheba, daughter of Amminadab, sister of Naashon, to wife; and she bare him Nadab, Abihu, Eleazar, and Ithamar.

Elisheba

From the ancient pearl beds
hidden deep in the Red Sea
the salty waters gave up pearls
possessing rare beauty that would
endure for generations to come

As written on pages of antiquity
Elisheba was blessed among
women— consecrated with a
rarity of motherhood that would
be praised for generations to come

Through her lineage in the tribe
of Levi came Elizabeth,
the mother of John the Baptist
Through her lineage in the tribe
of Judah came Mary,
the mother of Jesus Christ

Elisheba, a rarity of kinship—
a rarity of pearls

Claudia V. Camp, Jewish Women's Archive

Although her self-presentation as a mother is in one sense artifice, it also indicates an acknowledged source of women's authority and wisdom in ancient Israel

2 Samuel 14

Then the woman said, neither doth God respect any person: yet doth he devise means, that his banished be not expelled from him.

Tekoah Woman

In the eye of the beholder
the baroque pearl—

>with its irregularities
>in size and shape
>with its diminished
>value compared to the
>most perfectly round—

is still unique and beautiful

The nameless woman from
Tekoah was gifted and wise—
she was eloquent of speech
with irresistible and persuasive
words of pathos and poetry
that softened David's heart
to bring home his exiled son

If
the luster and glow of a pearl
emanates from within its heart—

then
how bright and beautiful is the
luster of the imperfect and
nameless woman from Tekoah

Acts 18:26

He began to speak boldly in the synagogue, but when Priscilla and Aquila heard him, they took him aside and explained to him the way of God more accurately.

Priscilla

While pearls can be matched
by man's design
no two have ever been declared
identical

Still, each mention of Priscilla's
name implied that she and her
husband were one and the same

Priscilla was considered as
Paul's dear and "fellow worker"
a teacher and faithful disciple—

when matched with Aquila

yet
much less considered
for the distinct authorship
of the Letter to the Hebrews—

as some believe she was

Was she denied this honor
by man's design
by the opinion that she *must* be
identical

Antiquities of the Jews IX vii 3
Flavius Josephus

Now when Athaliah, the daughter of Ahab, heard of the death of her brother Joram, and of her son Ahaziah, and of the royal family, she endeavored that none of the house of David might be left alive, but that the whole family might be exterminated, that no king might arise out of it.

Athaliah

Judah was the shell
The law was the oyster

Idolatry was the intruder—
entering to threaten and destroy
She was named Athaliah
Queen of Judah

Like the butterfly takes flight
in the face of autumn
Like the hummingbird attacks
in the face of danger
Like the oyster buries the intruder
in the face of destruction

Instinctively—
they wield their swords of survival
and go to battle

Prophetically—
the obedient wield their swords
to bury the murderous intruders

Gen. Rabbati, Vayeze, p. 120
Jewish Women's Archive

Jacob loved Rachel more than Leah and he even loved Rachel's handmaiden Bilhah more than Zilpah, Leah's handmaiden.

Bilhah

Near the Sea of Galilee—
where the warm blue waters
rush in to kiss the holy sand—
Bilhah lies as one of the
six matriarchs atTiberas

as one of the pearls
in Israel's sea chest—
the Tomb of the Matriarchs

Bilhah was matched in death
with

Jochebed, mother of Moses
Zipporah, wife of Moses
Elisheba, wife of Aaron
Abigail, wife of King David
Zilpah, Handmaid of Leah

Jacob loved Bilhah—
the timid handmaiden
She was matched in life
with

Rachel

Acts 16:16
New American Standard Bible

It happened that as we were going to the place of prayer, a slave-girl having a spirit of divination met us, who was bringing her masters much profit by fortune-telling......Paul..... turned and said to the spirit, In the name of Jesus Christ I command you to come out of her!

Nameless Slave-Girl

Witch
fortuneteller
demon possessed—

As in apostolic days
as in medieval days
as in colonial days—
as still today
behavior is more often
criticized than understood

much more sensational
with a scarlet letter
or a burning at the stake

Did she cry out in sorcery
or in fear of her own destiny
or— in the grip of occult powers

The writings of Luke
do not tell us of the
nameless slave-girl's fate

only
that Paul understood—
and she was set free

Acts of Paul and Thecla
The Christiaan Apocrypha

And Thecla said to them: "I am going to the city of Iconium." Paul saith to her: "Go and teach there the commandments of God."

Margaret Y. MacDonald says,

Even if Thecla's life is purely fictional, it remains significant that in second-century Pauline circles, a woman could be depicted as a teacher and evangelist in her own right....

Thecla

Some have proclaimed
Thecla a virgin, a saint
a teacher and evangelist

others—
a woman only story bound

But then
what of parables

    the mustard seed
    the lost sheep
    the faithful servants
    or
    the pearl

What of
    sacrifice and tribulation
    dedication and good works

whether by a man
or
a woman

Sirach 24:29, 33

For deeper than the sea are her thoughts, and her counsels.....

Proverbs 8:1, 14

Does not Sophia [wisdom] cry? and understanding put forth her voice?

Sophia Spirituality
    by Elaine Guillemin

Sophia can become a major connection between feminists and traditional churchgoers, between Christian, Jewish, and goddess-centered feminists, between historical and mythological worldviews, between the image of the hero and the image of the oppressed in history, art, and literature.

Sophia

The written words
began in Hebrew
then translated in
Greek, Latin, German
English et cetera, et cetera......

Sophia means wisdom
Margaret means pearl
Anna means grace
Sarah means princess
Rhoda means rose

Does the name signify
a woman
or an impression—
or both

Was Sophia
real or only a myth
was she
a feminist or a Christian
an activist or a messenger

Was Sophia
human or divine—
or both

1 Samuel 18:20-27 NIV

Now Saul's daughter Michal was in love with David, and when they told Saul, he was pleased.

2 Samuel 6:16 KJV

Michal Saul's daughter looked through a window, and saw king David......
and she despised him in her heart.

Michal

Michal professed her love
for David, and it was
written for all to witness

For the wrath of her
jealous father Saul
Michal let David down
through the open window
and he fled for his life

She laid an image of
pillow and goat's hair
in her husband's bed
to deceive her father—

Then
Michal professed her fear
of David— that she had lied
for his threat to her own life

and it was written for
all to witness

Like the warm and inviting
waters of a new pearling season
they soon turn cold and treacherous

Genesis 26:34-35

And Esau was forty years old when he took to wife Judith the daughter of Beeri the Hittite, and Bashemath the daughter of Elon the Hittite:

Adam Clarke's Commentary

Hence, we presume that in the course of the past forty-seven years she has died without male issue

Judith, the Hittite

One may glance at a
shiny pearl and think it
truly mother-of-pearl

unaware of the soft
wax hidden beneath
only a *powder of pearl*

polished to a luster

A closer look reveals
Judith, the Hittite
a worshipper of idols—

of false gods

Truth and law were
disregarded by Esau—
blinded by his bitterness
toward his brother—
and he took her for his wife

Yet
Judith was to him
a false and empty pearl

Romans 16:7

Salute Andronicus and Junia, my kinsmen and my fellow prisoners, who are of note among the apostles and who also were in Christ before me.

Rev. Kathryn A. Piccard, Episcopal Priest

Some scholars have translated her name as male – 'Junias' – but no such masculine name is found in any extant Greek or Latin document of the New Testament era.

The Pearl Source, Importer, Los Angeles

.....some pearls do not need manipulation or cutting in order to obtain the right appearance

Junia

Only the Creator can say
whether the creation has
the right appearance

If
the fruit is sweet
does it matter the tree

If
the deed is good
does it matter the gender

If
the pearl is lustrous
does it matter the color

Must Junia's worthiness
as a woman
be peeled away by ages
of speculation and bias
of interpretations— or *mis*

Perhaps the conclusion
for Saint Junia
lies only with the Creator

Peter Returns 1695
Woodcut by Johann Christoph Weigel

Act 12:13

Peter knocked at the outer entrance, and a servant named Rhoda came to answer the door. When she recognized Peter's voice, she was so overjoyed she ran back without opening it and exclaimed, "Peter is at the door!

Rhoda

To hear Peter's voice
at the door

to feel the sense of relief
in her heart

to rejoice that their prayers
had been answered

would be reason enough for
Rhoda's amusing exuberance

Hers was the privilege of being
the first to hear Peter's voice—
Rhoda, a simple servant girl

Although Weigel may have cut
Rhoda into the upper corner
of his composition—
he masterfully portrayed
her jubilant spirit with the
light of a brilliant torch
falling upon
her image

Judith Slaying Holofernes
Artemisia Gentileschi 1611-12
Oil on Canvas

Judith 8: 32
Old Testament of Catholic Bible

Judith said to them, "Listen to me. I am about to do a thing which will go down through all generations of our descendants

Mary Garrard, 1989

Although the painting depicts a classic scene from the Bible, Artemisia drew herself as Judith and Agostino Tassi, who was tried in court for her rape, as Holofernes.

Judith, the Courageous

The brush of many masters
has portrayed the face of
Judith with her known beauty

In her face

Donatello admired her virtue

Giorgione revealed her sexuality

Caravaggio captured her courage

Yet
it was *another woman*
Artemisia
who reached into the depths
of her soul—

revealing a sense of purpose
driven by virtue and loyalty
a strength greater than
the beheaded Holofernes
could ever have imagined

Perhaps Artemisia finally declared
her own power as a woman

Karen Kay Knauss

Karen is a native Oklahoman. She earned a Bachelor of Arts at the University of Science and Arts of Oklahoma, and has enjoyed careers as a teacher, musician, and artist. Her unique hand cast fiber sculptures are exhibited in public and private collections across the United States as well as in several foreign countries. She established Sundance Fine Arts Studios, performs in the vocal duo, Heart & Soul, and has devoted decades to the research of her family history.

Karen has authored four poetry collections, two poetry chapbooks, and she has co-authored two genealogical chronicles. She is an active member of several state poetry societies, and serves as Oklahoma Treasurer, as well as a competition Judge. Karen has received numerous awards for her poetry in statewide and national contests and was awarded Poet Laureate of the Poetry Society of Oklahoma.

works by   **Karen Kay Knauss**

OKLAHOMA COAL FIRES
Poetry Collection

The Thorny Truth and Their Civil War
Poetry Collection

77 Pieces of Poetry About Oklahoma
Poetry Collection

A Gathering of Pearls
Poetry Collection

Deep Blue Waters
Poetry Chapbook

Leaving *Flatland* by Poetry
Poetry Chapbook

Chronicles
KNAUSS FAMILY HISTORY
Co-Author, Kathleen Knauss McCullar

TRULL FAMILY HISTORY
Co-Author, Kathleen Knauss McCullar

www.ingramcontent.com/pod-product-compliance
Lightning Source LLC
Chambersburg PA
CBHW071118090426
42736CB00012B/1940